A Slightly Larger

Book of

Kick-Arse Poetry

About the Author

"I have a whole heap of qualifications and a stunning array of marvellous attributes - which you can look up if you're that keen, but frankly I wouldn't bother as they have absolutely nothing to do with my writing this book."

The Idea Factory
A division of I.C.E.P.S. Ltd.,
Wellington, New Zealand.

A Slightly Larger Book of Kick-Arse Poetry

Like my earlier book (*A Small Book of Kick-Arse Poetry*) this one is mostly written for 12-15 year olds who hate reading, but like its predecessor I suspect it will have a much wider readership.

This time there is a glossary at the back, so that you can look up any words you don't know. It's not like your average dictionary, though. Most dictionaries are about as much fun to read as the telephone directory. This dictionary will surprise you, and you may find yourself just reading through it, as though it was a series of 'posts' on a social networking site. Most teens who are poor readers don't like to look words up in the dictionary, because they are none the wiser having done so – too many definitions, too few examples, and just plain boring. The Kick-Arse dictionary will grab your attention, make you laugh, and hopefully burn the words onto your brain's hard drive.

The feedback from the first book was truly amazing: youngsters who wouldn't normally read anything other than the microwave instructions for their noodles, who devoured the book from start to finish, and then read it over again. It's worth it just for that. To become a proficient reader you need to read a lot. You need to read stuff that's more complex than microwave instructions. I just hope that some of those youngsters were inspired to read something else, and something else - but just in case they were having trouble finding a suitable something else I thought I'd write another book.

All of these poems are designed to stretch vocabulary. Most will make you laugh. Some will make you think about things, and talk about things. I had a blast writing them, and hope you enjoy reading them. L.E.J.

Copyright © 2013 by Lissa Elaine Judd

All rights reserved. This book or any portion thereof may not be reproduced or used in any manner whatsoever without the express written permission of the publisher except for the use of brief quotations in a book review.

International Edition
First printing November, 2013

ISBN: 978-0-473-26612-7

Also available:

Kindle Edition ISBN: 978-0-473-26611-0
Kindle apps from: www.amazon.com and www.amazon.co.uk
www.amazon.com.au (Australia & NZ sales)

Book website: www.anwyl.com/stuff
Facebook page: www.facebook.com/kickapoetry

enquiries to:
The Idea Factory
P.O. Box 57021 Mana
Porirua 5247
NEW ZEALAND
editor@anwyl.com

Contents

It wasn't me, Miss	6	The spot	43
Scrabble	7	Mary-Sue	45
Eddie	8	Three ladies in a chair	46
I'm the king around here	9	Eddie Noon	48
Ideas	10	Camping	51
Joy	10	Don't blame me	53
Fireworks	11	My birthday	55
My lunch	13	The Kimberley	57
Eat your tea	14	Uncle Adolf	58
Poetry assignment	15	Maths	59
The poo	17	My room	60
Voices	18	Uncle Willy	63
12/8 Blues	19	Chocolate	64
Hello cat	20	Christmas	66
My friend Martin	22	GLOSSARY	70
Grandpa Perkins	26		
The motel	29		
How come I can't have a pet?	30		
Happy days	32		
Not just a twit	33		
The parent-teacher meeting	35		
Little Onyx	37		
Kitty	38		
The essay	39		
Holiday at the beach	41		

It wasn't me, Miss

It wasn't me Miss it was him he started it -
he pushed me first,
he hurt my arm,
I didn't mean him any harm.
I told him he should lay off me and go and sit -
he wouldn't have a bar of it;
I know I'm not supposed to hit
him in the nose,
I don't suppose.

But Miss he called me names and stuff and said that I'm
a silly boy,
he took my pen,
I should have punched the bugger then.
I know I should ignore him Miss but all the time
he laughs at me the little swine.
I'm innocent of any crime.
I only hit
a little bit.

You see Miss there he goes again I didn't say
that stuff about
him being fat
and stinky too and things like that.
He's lying Miss, I didn't say that stuff today,
he's just pretending to look grey,
his nose was that shape anyway:
slightly bent,
with a dent.

Scrabble

I'm playing Scrabble with my dad -
he knows a lot of words,
like 'oo' and 'iwi' - what are those?
He says that they are birds.

My letters are all consonants -
I've Q, X, Z, and J,
and T and M and W
just add to my dismay.

My dad has just scored 50
with a double word score word.
I'll have to throw my letters out.
This game is just absurd.

But then I have a bright idea,
a way to get a score -
I spill my cocoa lavishly
and some goes on the floor.

My dad leaps from the table
and heads towards the sink.
He's gone to get a dampened cloth
to clean it up, I think.

But while he's gone I swap my X
and J for I and U,
and now I think I have a way
to use my T and Q.

I put my 'QUIT' against his S,
the Q's on triple letter -
the score is just enormous;
my total's looking better.

My father is ebullient,
and cheers at my success;
he's mopping up the cocoa still -
I've really made a mess.

With pangs of guilt for cheating thus,
I grab four letter tiles:
the J and X are back, I see;
my dad is still all smiles.

Eddie

Little Eddie on a dare,
tried to feed the polar bear.
He thought he was incredible;
the bear thought he was edible.

I'm the king around here

got a hole in my underpants
got nits in my hair
I can do armpit farts
I'm the king around here

I haven't any whiskers
only three pubic hairs
my legs are pretty skinny
but I'm the king around here

can't dance worth a shit
don't know what to wear
I've no particular talent
but I'm the king around here

my dad's a loser
drinks too much beer
hasn't got a job
I'm the king around here

when I leave school
I'll get me a career
don't know what I'll do
but I'm the king around here

Ideas

I wish that I could understand
the ideas
half formed, that wake me in the night,
ethereal visions, ripe
with meaning;
always just out of sight:
tiny mouse-like whispers,
almost heard,
softly cutting through my mind.
Ideas so important
they leave
no impression of any kind.

Joy

I drove the jet boat really fast
so Joy could water-ski.
We hit a log full throttle,
and sped on Joylessly.

Fireworks

Eric found some fireworks
in a box inside the shed,
and he grabbed a nice selection
which he hid beneath his bed.

He sent a text to all his friends
and asked them to come 'round -
he couldn't wait a minute more
to show them what he'd found.

His mum and dad had both gone out
to visit uncle Fred,
but Eric had the sniffles,
so he'd stayed at home instead.

His friends arrived, he let them in,
he knew they'd be impressed -
a box full of explosives never
fails to please your guests.

Their eyes lit up, they couldn't wait
to set the things alight.
"But wait," said one, "do you not think
this should be done at night?"

"No," said Eric firmly,
"my parents are away,
but they'll be home within the hour -
we really can't delay."

"We'll light them in the bathroom
so the neighbours do not see.
That Mrs Armstrong from next door
is always watching me."

So Eric let his fireworks off,
he'd had a bright idea -
he'd do it in the bathtub
so that water would be near.

It caused a conflagration,
and although Eric tried
to douse the fire with bathtub tap,
they sadly all got fried.

Mrs Armstrong saw the flames
and called the fire brigade.
The house burned down before the men
could come to Eric's aid.

My lunch

I ate my lunch a while ago;
I left my apple core.
It's gone all brown and manky -
it's not pretty any more.

I took it to my art class -
I put it on the floor;
I gave it half a turn,
then turned it a little more.

My teacher was ecstatic -
she said that it showed flair;
she swooned as she beheld
my apple core lying there.

She summonsed all the class
to come and gather 'round
to admire my apple core
lying there upon the ground.

She said it was symbolic -
imbued with heavy meaning:
simplistic in its form,
gargantuan in its leaning.

I said it was my lunch -
I put it on the floor;
it's gone all brown and manky -
it's really nothing more.

Eat your tea

My mum says that there are starving people in the world,
and I have to eat all my tea.
I wish those starving people would leave me alone.
They're here every night.
Except pizza night.
Starving people are happy to eat broccoli,
apparently,
and Brussels sprouts,
and Mum says I should be thankful and finish off
my parsnip.

Those starving people are sure annoying.
I don't bother them and tell them what to eat.
I leave those starving people alone,
wherever they are,
in Africa,
or sleeping in a car, or something.
I don't mess with them, every night.
Except pizza night.
Sure is a funny world
where starving people make me eat
my parsnip.

Poetry assignment

My dad's not home;
he drives a truck.
He's away a lot;
I don't give a toss.

He hits my mother
with his fist;
drinks beer and vodka
'til he's inebriated.

Me and Michael
try and stay
inside our room
out of his way.

We move the bed
against the door,
and crouch together
on the floor.

But just in case,
I've got a stick;
if he comes in,
I'll hit the swine.

Why does my mum
put up with it?
Why are we stuck
with all this difficulty?

I'll stick around
another year,
then me and Mike
are outa here.

*very good James,
but its "Michael and I",
and some of the verses don't rhyme.*

C+

The poo

I'm sitting on the toilet
and I'm starting to despair -
I'm trying to do a monster poo
but its stuck somewhere in there.

My mum has called me down to tea -
I said I won't be long.
She came and called a second time,
and asked if something's wrong.

"I'm fine," I said, "I'll be right there" -
I pushed with all my might.
I held my breath 'til I went blue -
this could go on all night.

It won't go back, it won't come out;
I pause to have a rest,
then push until my eyeballs bulge,
my knees against my chest.

It moved a tiny fraction,
but its starting to get sore.
My mum is getting anxious,
and she's knocking on the door.

"What are you doing? Are you ill?"
But it would sound absurd,
to tell my mum that I'm defeated
by a giant turd.

I squat upon the toilet seat
to see if this will help,
and finally it dislodges,
and I give a little yelp.

There's blood spots on the paper
and it hurts a lot inside -
but the poo is so enormous,
that I stare at it with pride.

Voices

voices floating on the wind
a fugue of unheard words
rising and falling
fading into the past
bright ripples of laughter
amidst turquoise baritone
softly caress my skin
breezy phrases with no meaning
staccato syllables unfelt
while sitting unnoticed in the crowd
listening
to the silent dancer in my head.

$^{12}_{8}$ Blues

why am I
trying to
work it out
work it out

difficult
road ahead
in my head
going to

dar es salaam
better than
where I am
in my mind

will I find
sanity
will I be
rid of this

manic crow
talons sharp
gripping my
pounding heart

when can I
make a start
down the road
in my head

where is that
house of peace
welcome place
warm embrace

and at last
silken sleep
ocean deep
suffocates

fear
fear
fear
fear

Hello cat

Hello cat,
can I sit here?
It's you and me
alone, I fear.

I'm home from school,
I've got the 'flu;
I have to spend
the day with you.

My throat is sore.
Does yours hurt too?
There really isn't
much to do.

You don't say much,
but that's okay;
we can talk
another day.

Do you play cards?
I've got a set.
I wonder if it's
lunch time yet.

Would you like
an apricot?
You say you don't
eat those a lot?

I've also got
a bit of cake,
but now I have
a stomach ache.

You can have it
if you wish.
I'll go and get
your dinner dish.

You didn't eat it -
are you ill?
Perhaps you'd like
to have my pill?

You're not much fun,
I have to say;
you sure you wouldn't
like to play?

Have you heard
a word I've said?
You still feel warm;
you can't be dead.

Well here we are
just you and me.
You say you need
to take a pee?

You're off outside?
Well, that's okay.
I hope you have
a lovely day.

There really isn't
much to do.
No one will be
home 'til two.

These matches make
a lovely flame;
this is a most
amusing game.

My word those books
burn really bright!
I bet my mum
will get a fright.

My friend Martin

Martin's got a broken arm;
he fell out of a tree.
He reckons that I pushed him -
I said it wasn't me.
He'd hit his head,
we'd thought him dead,
we'd felt it best if we all fled,
and left him torpidly.

But Martin found an inner strength,
and rose up from the ground.
"You bloody bastards!" Martin said,
when no one could be found.
"I hurt like hell,
I don't feel well,
I smashed my cell phone when I fell
and landed on this mound!"

Poor Martin made the journey home,
blood streaming down his face;
he now had double vision,
so he hoped he'd find the place.
His right arm hurt,
he'd torn his shirt,
and caked in blood and twigs and dirt -
his clothes were a disgrace.

When he got home his mum was shocked -
she called out for his dad,
who drove him to the doctor,
to straighten out the lad.
His nose was bent,
his shirt was rent,
and in his skull - a giant dent,
and his arm was broken bad.

The doctor gave him medicine
to take away the pain -
it made poor Martin queasy,
and he vomited again.
They stitched his head
where it had bled
(and stained his shirt a cherry red,
much to his mum's disdain).

The doctor tugged upon his arm
until the bones aligned;
they checked it with an x-ray,
while Martin wailed and whined.
It's in a cast
to hold it fast
until the bones repair at last -
six weeks, I think you'll find.

But I've gone into hiding,
'coz Martin told his dad
his injuries were all my fault -
his dad was hopping mad!
I'm innocent,
I only meant
to slap his back when Martin went
all blue and coughing bad.

He coughed and wheezed and spluttered
and I thought that he would choke,
so I thumped him firmly to dislodge
the thing stuck in his throat.
I gave a whack
and he fell back
and now I'm blamed for his attack:
I tried to save the bloke!

Well yes, we left him in the rain -
we probably should have stayed.
We thought he was a goner;
we really were dismayed.
A policeman came -
he had my name;
he seemed to think I was to blame
for leaving him where he laid.

My friends are dubbed accomplices,
for helping in my crime
of leaving Martin lying there
amid the muck and grime.
We didn't stay.
We have to pay
a fine or go to jail today
and stay there quite some time.

Oh, the dread ignominy
of having to pay a fine.
I should've let the bugger choke -
ungrateful little swine!
He should have said
he'd hurt his head,
and not pretended to be dead;
he is no friend of mine.

Grandpa Perkins

Grandpa Perkins can get lost
when walking down the street -
he asks directions frequently
from people he should meet.

Trouble is, he can't remember
where he's going to,
or where he's from, or who he is,
or what he's going to do.

Grandma always worries that
he'll wander far away;
she's placed a name tag 'round his neck
in case he strays today.

Last week she found him digging
in a neighbour's veggie plot,
and he took some persuading
that his house, this was not.

He'd tied up the tomatoes,
and picked a crop of peas,
and dug up the potatoes,
despite my grandma's pleas.

But Pops was always cheerful,
and he'd really no idea
of the panic he created
as his family wondered where

on Earth he might have got to -
which direction had he taken?
Oblivious to all of this,
his faculties forsaken,

he'd wander into foreign lands
he'd never seen before -
completely unfamiliar
even though it was next door;

and people whom he'd never met
would greet him by his name,
and ring up Grandma on their phone,
and wait until she came.

But one day Grandpa wandered off,
but this time no one saw
the old man trudging mindlessly,
as he had done before.

He walked for hours, without a care,
but now he's getting cold -
he looks about with some concern;
he's tired and feeling old.

He's left behind suburbia,
he's lost amidst the trees.
Poor Grandpa Perkins sits a while,
and rubs his aching knees.

It's getting late, the light is dim,
and Pops is gripped with fear -
he cannot fathom whether home
is far away, or near.

Now he feels some urgency
to reach his destination.
The rain's set in, he notices,
with some disapprobation.

The going's rough, the light has gone -
he really should take care,
but Grandpa Perkins trips and falls,
and now he's lying there.

His bones are thin, his hip has broke,
his clothes are soaked with rain.
He wished he'd brought his overcoat,
or something for the pain.

Grandma was beside herself-
she'd hunted high and low;
she'd telephoned authorities,
and everyone she knows.

Neighbours, friends, and family,
with thermos flasks of soup,
arrived to help poor Grandma,
and form a searching group.

Donning rainproof outerwear
for their own protection,
they all set off earnestly,
in the wrong direction.

So Grandpa Perkins' last adventure
ended on that day:
no one came to rescue him,
to Grandma's great dismay.

The motel

Four old ladies in the pool,
splashing about,
floating on their backs
like brightly coloured potatoes.
Young man dives in handsomely,
glides past,
faster than his shorts -
pink cheeks surfacing
amongst the manatee mermaids
giggling like young girls.

How come I can't have a pet?

All my friends have got a pet:
a cat or dog,
Australian frog,
a lizard sleeping on a log -
so how come I've not got one yet?

An elephant would be so cool -
we could play
every day.
It really won't be in the way -
and I could ride it to my school.

But Mum, I'll keep it really clean!
It won't smell,
I can tell;
I'll scrub it really really well.
I think you're being awfully mean!

It will not scare the neighbour's cat!
It won't bite,
or cause a fright,
or trumpet loudly in the night -
it won't do anything like that!

I'll teach him how to come when called,
and how to sit,
and all that shit.
You say you're having none of it?
You say that frankly you're appalled?

He will not squash my brother Jim!
He won't drop hair,
or break the chair,
and no, he won't poop everywhere!
Of course I will look after him!

You say you're being really firm?
You will not let
me have a pet,
and certainly I cannot get
a tree-uprooting pachyderm?

But Mum, you're being so unfair!
I'll run away;
I cannot stay.
I never liked you anyway!
I'm going to relocate from here.

I paused to let my threat sink in,
then slammed the door,
and stomped the floor,
and shouted idle threats some more.
I wish just once that I could win,

'coz all my friends have got a pet,
except for Jim,
and Steve and Tim,
and Connor, Dennis, Ben and Kim -
so how come we've not got one yet?

Happy days

maths class
can't pass
dumb arse
won't go
who'll know?
sneak out
three of us
easy as
Jim has
money for
take-aways
happy days
pass time
big store
games galore
Xbox
outfox
pocket one
its done
so shrewd
nabbed by
store guy
Dad called
Mum appalled
police cell
funny smell
lonely wait
God, I hate
maths class
dumb arse

Not just a twit

My schoolbag's full of chocolate cake,
and nutty toffee slice,
a thermos full of homemade soup,
and other stuff that's nice.

My mum thinks I've an appetite -
I ask for more and more
of lunchtime sweets and savouries
and food that I adore.

I don't get any bigger -
I'm as skinny as a rake.
Mum marvels that I don't get fat
with all this food I take.

The fried rice is a favourite,
and laksa chicken curry,
but I just raid the biscuit tins
if Mum is in a hurry.

There are no classes at my school
in which I can excel.
My teachers think I'm stupid, and
in life I won't do well.

But I've a special talent
of which they're unaware -
a good business acumen and
entrepreneurial flare.

At lunch I make a fortune
selling curry, soup and rice -
two dollars for a savoury,
and one for cake and slice.

My reading is abysmal and
my maths is pretty poor,
but I can add the takings
and I've twenty dollars more.

So sucks to all the teachers
who didn't have the wit
to notice I had assets
and wasn't just a twit.

The parent-teacher meeting

Mum has bought a stripey hat.
I thinks she's mad -
she looks a prat;
I sure hope that she won't wear that
to the parent-teacher meeting.

My parents meet me at the school,
she's worn the hat -
I feel a fool;
I sure hope Dad won't lose his cool
at the parent-teacher meeting.

Every teacher that we see
agrees I've no
ability
or skill, as far as they can see,
at the parent-teacher meeting.

They say I don't try hard enough -
I just give up
when things get tough.
They tell my parents all this stuff
at the parent-teacher meeting.

I sit there trying not to care:
(the stripey hat -
my friends all stare.)
Opprobrium is all I hear
at the parent-teacher meeting.

My English teacher tells my dad
that I'm the worst
she's ever had;
she said I'm just a naughty lad,
at the parent-teacher meeting.

But Dad said this was all a farce,
and she was not
a teacher's arse.
This was heard by all my class,
at the parent-teacher meeting.

It's kind of like this every year -
ignominy
abounds, I fear.
I wish that I could disappear
at the parent-teacher meeting.

Little Onyx

Little Onyx, black and tan,
a Kelpie cross, and smaller than
his room-mate Iggy: Doberman.

Iggy's old and fairly slow,
while Onyx is always on the go,
and chasing balls and sticks I throw.

He goes like hell, he's always busy,
'round and 'round 'til Iggy's dizzy.
Now I've lost him. Gosh, where is he?

There he is, he's trying to herd
the neighbours' cats - its too absurd.
I called him back, but he demurred.

No, here he comes, as fast as light:
his ears are pricked, his eyes are bright,
while Iggs has got his eyes closed tight

as he lies there upon the ground
pretending to be not around
as Onyx clears him with one bound

and leaps straight up and knocks me flat -
I hadn't quite expected that.
He licks my face. I feel a prat.

But now he's off to have some fun -
can he get Iggs to play and run,
and frolic gaily in the sun?

He's patting Iggy on the nose -
he must like danger, I suppose,
for all of a sudden Iggy rose,

all fifty kilos, on his feet,
and for his age - surprisingly fleet
as he chased Onyx down the street.

Kitty

soft fur
little purr
tummy tickle
kitty cuddle
found a puddle
little paws
sharp claws
super fast
elastoplast

The essay

I have to write an essay
but the paper stays all white -
I stared at it for ages, but
can't think of stuff to write.

I'm focused on the task in hand,
I've everything I need;
I concentrate with all my might
until my forehead bleeds.

But still there are no hieroglyphs,
no markings on the page;
my pen won't do a bloody thing!
I'm filling up with rage.

What a stupid pen this is -
my essay's due today!
I want to get it finished now,
so I can go and play.

I look across at Stinky Jones
whose page is full of text;
his lips are moving quickly, reading
what his pen writes next.

My pen is still, it will not write,
it's mute, and I suppose,
that nothing that I do or say
will make the thing write prose.

Then comes an epiphany -
I realise what is wrong:
my ballpoint is a drawing pen -
it's been that all along.

And so I draw a picture,
filled with complex line and shade -
a stunning composition:
the best I've ever made.

Now that I am finished
I regard the thing with pride;
my teacher's not so satisfied
and makes me stay inside.

Holiday at the beach

We spent our summer by the sea -
I went with my whole family.
My dad had found a bach to rent -
we wouldn't all fit in the tent.

We head off to the beach next day:
me and brothers Mike and Ray.
We swim and frolic in the sun:
we've hours and hours and hours of fun.

We buried our brother in the sand -
it didn't go quite as we planned:
when we went to look for him,
we found meanwhile the tide came in.

I wondered how we'd tell our mother
that we had lost our little brother.
We knew she'd be as mad as hell
if this is what we had to tell.

As Mike and I gazed out to sea
a sharp idea occurred to me:
we'd say our brother caught the bus -
he's gone back home, he wants no fuss.

We must return here late at night.
We'll bring some shovels and a light,
so we can find and bury Ray -
I hope he hasn't washed away.

We got home late, as night set in;
mum glared at us across her gin.
"Where have you been? I want a word."
(She used that tone I often heard.)

She banged her glass down on the desk -
it overflowed and made a mess.
"You left your little brother Ray -
so what do you two have to say?"

Mike gave a gulp, I grabbed his arm;
he looked quite pale, while I stayed calm.
"He caught the bus, he'll be okay;
he really didn't want to stay."

'Twas well rehearsed, our web of lies,
but mum replied, to my surprise:
"Don't be silly, he's in bed,
his sunburned face is very red."

"Dad found him buried in the sand,
he had no hat, he wasn't tanned -
he's quite upset, his face is sore,
and swollen, blistered, red and raw."

"You should have watched your little brother -
kept an eye on one another,
but you two left to have some fun -
you're grounded 'til you're twenty one."

The spot

I cannot go to school today -
I've got a spot.
Oh, can't you see?
a thing of such enormity?
I kid you not
I cannot go!
I'll stay at home and watch it grow.

A second one has just appeared -
it's on my nose,
it's big and red,
it's grown bigger than my head.
I don't suppose
that if I pray
that both these spots will go away?

Of course my friends will notice them!
How can they not?
They'll laugh and stare -
embarrassment I cannot bear:
ignoble spot!
The outlook's bleak:
these things are going to last the week.

No they can't be covered up!
Are you mad?
They're way too large
to cover up with camouflage.
I've never had
a spot so huge.
They will not go with subterfuge.

I'll get a magnifying glass -
you must be blind!
Now do you see?
Oh God, another! Now there's three!
You cannot find
these grotesque lumps? -
these pestilential acne bumps?

Okay I'll use concealer cream.
You just don't care.
You're really mean.
And no, I'm not a drama queen!
It's so unfair!
Humiliation!
I'll surely die from denigration.

Mary-Sue

Mary-Sue's a pretty girl.
I idolise her every curl,
her dancing eyes, her laughter clear;
she doesn't even know I'm here.

I smile at her, she doesn't see.
She really doesn't notice me.
She looks straight past, to Jimmy Barnes
who sits behind with folded arms.

Jimmy's tall with facial hair -
the girls all swoon when he draws near.
But Jimmy has no charm or wit -
he is a most annoying git.

I wish that I was bold enough
to say 'hello' and all that stuff,
but I'm too scared to talk to her -
my heart-rate soars, my mind's a blur.

But then one day my dream comes true:
approaching me is Mary-Sue;
she purred at me, these silken words:
"Your fly's undone, you little nurd."

Three ladies in a chair

I'm feeling peckish in the night -
I creep downstairs, turn on the light
and there, reclining on my right:
three ladies in a chair.

I stare at them with some surprise -
I cannot quite believe my eyes
and none of them proselytise -
I know not why they're here.

They seem relaxed and quite at ease,
they've cups of tea, and bread and cheese;
the cat is sleeping on their knees -
they're quite at home, I fear.

I would've worn a dressing gown
if I had known when I came down
I'd find three ladies in my lounge:
I'm feeling rather bare.

I tried to strike a fearsome pose
while standing in my underclothes
demanding that these so and so's
remove themselves from there.

"But," said one, "we've every right -
we come and sit here every night.
We didn't mean to cause a fright."
She wiped away a tear.

"Our friend the cat unlocks the door -
he said that you were such a bore
at night, when all you do is snore."
She paused to stroke his ear.

At this, the cat rose up and said:
"I think you should go back to bed,
I'll let my guests out when they're fed."
He fetched them some eclairs.

He filled the ladies' cups with tea
and chatted to them amiably,
but not another word to me.
I thought it wasn't fair.

Each night since I'd lie awake
and wonder if they're eating cake;
a talking cat, for goodness sake,
and three ladies in a chair.

Eddie Noon

Eddie Noon -
he's in my class,
he slipped and fell
upon his arse.

His cellphone smashed -
it cut his bum;
the teacher went
and called his mum.

They took him off
to stitch his cut,
and put a bandage
on his butt.

Eddie's back
in school next day;
he stood for maths
he stood for play.

Eddie stood
the whole day long -
his bum too sore
to sit upon.

The rest of us
would chant and sing
that Eddie stood
for everything.

We joked (to add
to his torment)
"Why don't you stand
for President?"

But Eddie Noon
just stood his ground
he always smiled,
he never frowned.

Poor Eddie often
comes to harm -
last year it was
a broken arm.

The year before
he hit his head -
he lost some teeth,
his forehead bled.

It never seems
to bother him -
he always wears
a silly grin.

He was concussed
when he was ten,
and he's been grinning
ever since then.

Concussion injured
Eddie's brain-
its not been quite
the same again.

So, Eddie's gone
a little queer,
he's stitches in
his derriere.

His balance is
not very good -
he slips and falls
more than he should.

I don't think he'll
be sitting soon -
a bus has hit
poor Eddie Noon.

Camping

We're camping in the Aussie bush;
it's called 'the dry',
I don't know why -
its rained each day, there's no blue sky.

The rain has got in everywhere:
my bedding's wet,
and I can't get
my clothes or towel to dry out yet.

We can't get out, the road is closed;
of all the luck,
it's turned to muck,
the four wheel drive will just get stuck.

We pass the time by playing cards -
they're sodden too,
alas it's true,
there's really not much else to do.

I wish my bug-spray hadn't leaked
into my bag -
it's all I had;
the itchy bites will drive me mad.

There's tree frogs living in the loo,
and in my tent
a python went,
when I forgot to zip the vent.

The sand has got into the food -
it tastes of grit;
the cooking's shit -
I really can't eat much of it.

But we'll come back again next year.
We've had a blast,
it didn't last -
the time went by so very fast.

Don't blame me

Of course I didn't drink your beer -
I can't explain
why once again
it's disappeared, and none remain -
I really do have no idea.

You say you have the evidence?
The empties in
the wheelie bin,
and what remains of mother's gin?
You say it starts to all make sense?

And no, of course I do not smoke!
I could not get
some cigarettes -
I'm way too young to buy them yet,
and anyway, you know I'm broke.

What do you mean you've seen the butts?
Well, they're not mine.
You're out of line -
you always blame me all the time!
These accusations drive me nuts.

The freezer door was left ajar?
Well why blame me?
Did you not see
I went to bed straight after tea?
I really think you go too far.

You say the ice cream has all gone?
You think I might
(you're sure you're right)
have scoffed it all in dead of night?
You know that you cannot be wrong?

I lacked a cogent argument:
"You're not my dad !"
was all I had;
I stomped off feeling really bad.
I knew defeat was imminent.

My birthday

For my birthday in three weeks
I'd like, if that's okay,
a laptop for my schoolwork -
I'll use it every day.

All my friends have got one and
I'm really really sure
that it's the only thing I need -
I'll want for nothing more.

I know that they're expensive
but I've had this great idea:
I'll forego Christmas presents,
and my birthday gift next year.

I'm absolutely certain and
I will not change my mind.
You say I do that every year?
I think that's most unkind.

Mum, you know how I said that
a laptop would be good
for my birthday present in two weeks,
well now I think I should

have an iPad for my gift instead.
I've given it much thought.
They're easier to carry,
and I really think you ought

to give consideration to
this marvellous idea.
I will not change my mind again -
I'm definite, I swear.

Mum, my birthday's in one week,
and you know how I said
that I would like an iPad,
well there's something else instead:

just give me birthday money,
and don't buy me any stuff.
I'm sure five hundred dollars should
be just about enough.

You say I'll get a hundred
and there won't be any more?
Okay, I'll give my gran a ring -
she'll give me some I'm sure.

The Kimberley

We're camping in the Kimberley:
the days are really hot.
My hat fell in the long-drop -
the only hat I've got.

My clothes were pretty stinky
and the dust had stained them red;
I washed and hung them out to dry
before I went to bed.

But overnight a dingo came -
it was his lucky day,
'coz last night I forgot to put
the rubbish bag away.

The chicken bones and plastic wraps
have made a messy feast -
there's paper strewn everywhere
by this nocturnal beast.

But then to add to my dismay
my socks had disappeared;
he'd chewed a hole in my underpants -
it's worse than I had feared.

The washing bucket's in the grass,
the dishcloth is in shreds;
the bugger ate my toothpaste,
while we were in our beds.

But never mind, I've extra socks,
my underpants are airy;
I've draped the tea-towel over my head -
my outlook is still cheery.

Uncle Adolf

Uncle Adolf came to tea
to spend time with my family.
He brought us fruit and little cakes -
they're nicer than the ones mum makes.

He told us jokes, did magic tricks;
we played a game of pick-up-sticks.
He did the dishes after tea;
he's loved by all the family.

I asked him why the Jews all died -
why were they killed with cyanide?
"You wicked boy!" my mother spat,
"upsetting nice Uncle Alf like that."

Maths

If a train is heading north
at sixty kilometers an hour,
and a man is running in the train,
with all his eggs in one basket -
how fast are the eggs going?
"Why is the man running?
Is there a fire?
Are they free range eggs,
like mum gets?"

Mr Snodgrass says I should be quiet,
and do the sums.

"But if we run in the train,
on the way to school,
the guard says: 'stop running, you little snots,
or I'll throw you off.'
Are they brown eggs, or white?"

Mr Snodgrass says: 'don't be smart.'

But if I was smart,
I'd know why the man was running,
with a basket of eggs.

I draw a nice picture of a train.
That has to count for something.

My room

You say I have to clean my room?
Perhaps tonight
I think I might
have time to move things out of sight.
You say you want it done real soon?

I don't know how to make the bed,
or fold my clothes,
I don't suppose
that you could show me then I'd know.
"Don't be silly" mother said.

"I want your clothes up off the floor,
and in the wash,
and oh, my gosh!
What is this putrid thing that's squashed,
and hidden here behind the door?"

"So this is where the cups have gone!
And that plate there
is growing hair -
it's too revolting to go near.
How can you live amongst this pong?"

"Is this a school assignment here,
amidst the stack
of pizza packs,
and empty cans and bric-a-brac?"
(her voice was rising now, I fear)

I thought my room looked pretty swell.
The piles are neat,
there's room for feet;
an eclectic mix of things to eat.
It had a slightly boyish smell.

But Mum (I did protest at last) -
I'm still in bed.
I know you said
that I should clean my room instead,
but it's only two, perhaps half past.

I didn't go to bed 'til four.
It's way too soon
to clean my room.
I'll do it in the afternoon.
You surely can't expect much more.

(She took a quite aggressive pose)-
"Right now, young man,
or else you can
go kiss goodbye to your birthday plans."
(and other threats I won't disclose.)

So, I arose with humour foul,
and in a funk
surveyed the junk,
and grabbed the stuff that really stunk:
some rotting food, and mouldering towel.

I felt that I'd been put upon,
but forged ahead,
when mother said:
"My God! I see you went to bed
fully dressed and your shoes still on!"

(Her eyes now slits; she's pursed her lips)-
"Your sheets are torn
(she said with scorn),
and look at the state of the clothes you've worn!"
(She's standing now with hands on hips.)

But Mum, I try to do my best
to leave things be,
so naturally
my room will head towards entropy
and create domestic wilderness.

You should be proud of my attempt
to be so green,
and never clean
this habitat, that's so pristine.
It does not merit your contempt!

Uncle Willy

holiday
far away
family went
in a tent
Uncle Willy
very silly
toilet been
didn't clean
germy paws
he ignores
hygiene
bad scene
in the night
sad plight
tummy trouble
on the double
to the loo
do a poo
then it's worse
what a curse
had a chuck
bad luck
Uncle Willy
very silly
too late
denture plate
down the dunny
very funny

Chocolate

I put some chocolate in my bag -
it seemed a good idea,
but then the day warmed up a bit,
and it's gone everywhere.

There's chocolate on my essay and
my brand new science book;
my pens are now all sticky
-it's everywhere I look.

I licked it off my fingers and
I brushed it through my hair;
I wiped my pens upon my shirt -
I'm starting to despair.

I have to hand my essay in.
I tried to wipe it clean -
this smeared the chocolate onto where
clean page hitherto had been.

"I'm sorry, Mrs Wotherspoon."
(I handed in my work:
a chocolate coated essay -
boy I felt a jerk.)

She peered at it with narrowed eyes,
the way that teachers do.
"What's this?" my teacher said, at length;
she licked her fingers too.

And glumly we surveyed the thing:
small colonies of words,
marooned amidst a chocolate sea:
a pastiche too absurd.

"My homework, Mrs Wotherspoon.
I'm sorry that it's late.
I hope you'll find some merit in
my essayist's debate."

"So, you think the work discursive?
(and her tone was pretty cool)
Its more like a confection!
You can stay in after school."

Christmas

It's Christmas day, it's raining and
we're loading up the car.
We're having lunch at Gran's this year;
it isn't very far.

We have to set off early though -
Mum's got the whole thing planned:
we'll swoop in like the S.A.S.
to give the gran a hand.

She's barking orders at my dad,
to put things here and there;
he pays her no attention,
and he's gone to get the beer.

The boot is full of presents,
and a crate or two of booze;
I think I'll leave them to it,
and just have a little snooze.

At Gran's it's all unloaded -
we've got turkey, ham, and cake,
and lots of little Christmas pies
I watched my mother make.

The turkey takes a while to cook -
it goes in straight away.
We'd stuffed it with the stuffing that
my gran made yesterday.

My mum helps do the vegetables,
my dad surveys the tree;
I count up all the presents that
appear to be for me.

My sister's found the lollies
and she's eaten quite a few;
the trouble is, at Gran's there's really
nothing else to do.

Uncle Tom and Aunty Mary
pull up in the drive;
the table's set, the work's all done
before these rels arrive.

"Oh dear" says Aunty Mary,
"have we arrived too late?"
(she'd timed it very carefully:
they'd waited at the gate.)

She plumped herself down in a chair:
"I'll keep out of your way.
Tom, be a luv and bring a glass
of their cheap chardonnay."

Gran had lost her glasses -
she was hunting everywhere;
Dad and Pops retreated to
the garage with a beer.

I sneaked a little vodka
in my orange - just a tot;
I was stuck with cousin Ollie -
an annoying little snot.

We opened up the presents
and I got (to my disdain)
a waterproof red jacket,
to keep away the rain.

Grandma opened Uncle Tom's -
she couldn't read the name;
she thanked my Aunty Mary
for the Y-fronts, just the same.

We then sat down for Christmas lunch -
an enormous turkey feast;
and Grandma found her glasses had
been stuffed inside the beast.

I sneaked another vodka
to impart a rosey hue
to the Christmas day proceedings
-okay, so I had two....

then even cousin Ollie
seemed an entertaining wit;
we sang some Christmas carols,
and all that sort of shit.

And then the day is over and
we pack up all our stuff.
"I'll just have one more beer" says dad.
Mum says: "You've had enough."

We drive off home, it isn't far,
but on the way - a cop:
"Could you count to ten please sir."
But Dad found he could not.

GLOSSARY

Although some words have multiple meanings, I have usually only provided one meaning - the one used in the text.

I have shown you how to say each word, but not in the way that dictionaries usually do. The bit that is **<u>bold and underlined</u>** is the bit of the word which has the emphasis. Below are a few common words, and their pronounciation, to give you the hang of the thing.

beginning	be **<u>gin</u>** ning
elephant	**<u>el</u>** a funt
geography	jee **<u>og</u>** ruff fee
giraffe	ja **<u>rarf</u>**
sister	**<u>siss</u>** ter
tomato	tom **<u>ma</u>** toe
underlined	un der **<u>lined</u>**

abysmal   a **<u>biz</u>** mill
Really bad. Absolute crappo. Not to be confused with 'abyss', which is a really deep hole - so deep you can't see the bottom. However, if you fall into an abyss, this is really bad - that is to say: abysmal.

accomplice   a **<u>kom</u>** pliss
Someone who helps someone else commit a crime.

acumen	**ack** you men
	The ability to make good decisions. Usually refers to business, as in 'business acumen'. If you lack in business acumen, your business doesn't make much profit, and you may end up owing a lot of people money.
aligned	a **lined**
	In a straight line, or in the correct positions.
amiably	**amy** a blee
	In a friendly way.
argument	**ar** gew ment
	Reason or reasons; the way you try and persuade someone that what you think, or what you want to do is right. If they don't agree with you they may get angry and shout, and then you shout back, and now you're having a different sort of argument.

"Stinky Jones thought he had come up with a reasonable argument for not going to school anymore. He voiced his considered opinion to his parents, who listened with some interest."

Using the alternative meaning of 'argument' one might say: "Mr Jones, on learning that Stinky refused to go to school, flew into a rage. There was much shouting on both sides, and the argument carried on for an hour or more, until Stinky stomped off to sulk in his room."

assets	**ass** sets
	Useful things. Talents. "One of Stinky Jones' many assets, was his ability to do armpit farts."
baritone	**barry** tone
	A male voice that's not really deep like some guys, but not high and squeeky like other guys.
bric-a-brac	**brick** a brack
	A collection of things of little value, like you might find at a garage sale. Miscellaneous old tat.
camouflage	**kam** a flarge
	Disguise, cover up, blend into the surroundings.
Chardonnay	**shard** nay
	A white wine.
cogent	**ko** jent
	Clear and logical. One is usually talking about a discussion - your explanation makes good sense. "Coz its not fair" is not a cogent argument.
concussion	kon **kush** shun
	When the lights go out briefly after a blow to the head; losing consciousness for a bit.

confection	kon **feck** shun	

confection   kon **feck** shun
A sweet food, like pudding or lollies - particularly if its a bit fancy or special. You wouldn't usually use this word to describe your mum's apple crumble, unless she does it really fancy like an expensive restaurant.

conflagration   kon fla **gray** shun
A big fire that spreads over a big area.

contempt   kon **tempt**
See 'disdain'. You not only don't like it, it's insulting. Only your impeccable manners stops you from giving them a good slap. Like when your mum suggests that you could take your little sister with you to the skate park - you treat this idea with the contempt it deserves. (But don't slap you mother, no matter how contemptuous the suggestion, or you'll be in deep shit for a long time.)

Dar es Salaam
    dar es sa **lahm**
A big city in Tanzania, Africa. In Arabic it means: a place of peace.

demurred   de **murd** [rhymes with turd]
Showed reluctance, wasn't keen. "Gran asked Ollie if he would like to taste her pickled fish, but he demurred."

denigration	denny **gray** shun To denigrate means to criticise unfairly, like when you're referred to as 'a little snot'. Denigration is the criticism - the mean, unfair words that are slung at you.
derriere	dear ay [rhymes with hay] **er** Bum, butt.
digress	die **gress** Change the subject. You are talking about how to trick Stinky Jones into eating a chilli sandwich, and then, for a few minutes, you discuss hippos, and then back onto Stinky Jones. The hippo discussion was a digression from the main topic. Having gone off course onto hippos, you might say apologetically "But I digress" and then resume your discussion of tactics to plant a chilli sandwich in Stinky's lunchbox.
disapprobation	dis ap pro **bay** shun Disapproval. "Risking his mother's disapprobation, Ollie hid his soiled underpants, along with last week's leftover pizza, under the bed."
discursive	dis **curse** iv This has two meanings. It can mean hopping about from one subject to another; going off at

a tangent. You start banging on about a movie you saw last night, digress on to what you had for tea, and end up talking about some girl on the train.

On the other hand, it can mean that your discussion of something proceeds in a logical fashion. You make your case like some flash lawyer.

What kind of crazy word is this, that means opposite things? It means rambling and disordered, but it also means logical and ordered !

So, a discursive argument for being allowed to go to your friend Michael's party, could be a good one, and your parents will reply: "OK that sounds reasonable", or it could be the desperate incoherent ramblings of an idiot and they'll say: "over my dead body." But, if they do say that, you can always respond: "So, you think my argument discursive?" They may get confused and let you go anyway.

disdain	dis **dain**
	See 'contempt'. If you regard something with disdain, it means you don't like it - it's an insult - like broccoli, or what your mum thinks is a 'really smart shirt'.

dislodges dis **lodj** ez
Removes from somewhere. "Ollie had a large beetle stuck up his nose, but he finally dislodges it with a big sneeze - it shoots out of his nostril and lands in his sister's breakfast cereal. Mistaking it for a large raisin, she scoops it up in her spoon and swallows it."

dismayed dis **maid**
Upset. "Stinky Jones was dismayed to find a dead frog in his gumboot."

douse **dowse**
Pour liquid over. Put out a fire. "Mrs Jones, on discovering the cat was generously covered in blackcurrant jam, doused it with the hose. This resulted in a jammy, wet, bad-tempered cat, and 'ebullient' was not a word which would get within a hundred metres of Mrs Jones."

dubbed **dubd**
A nickname. "Jeremiah Jones was dubbed 'Stinky' by his mates, because his real name was stupid."

ebullient ih [rhymes with pip] **bew** lee ent
Cheerful and happy. "Having set fire to his trousers, the ebullient Eddie Noon grinned his best and biggest grin, blissfully happy that he wasn't wearing them at the time"

eclectic	ee **klek** tick

This word could refer to things, or to styles, and it means that they're a bit of a jumble. An eclectic taste in music means that you have folk, rock, and Chinese opera on your iPod.

enormity	ee **norm** it tee

Big, huge, serious. "With his trousers burnt to ashes and no money for the bus, Eddie Noon pondered the enormity of the situation"

entropy	**en** trup pee

Random, disordered.

entrepreneurial

on trah prah **nor** ee al

An entrepreneur is this dude who seems to be able to make a dollar out of anything. Such a dude is said to be entrepreneurial - but you'll never be able to pronounce it so just say 'clever dick' or 'hustler'.

epiphany	ih [rhymes with pip] **piff** a nee

A revelation. Suddenly, you've got it. The answer comes to you with a wham, like a blow to the head with a cricket ball (and often with similar stars and bright flashes of light).

essayist	**ess** say ist

One who writes essays.

ethereal	ee **there** ['th' as in 'thick'] ee al Delicate, light, perfect, as though from some magical or spiritual world.
faculties	**fak** cull tees Mental or physical powers or talents. "Ollie's faculties were sufficiently blunted by the effects of several vodkas, that he decided, in this inebriated state, that it would be a good idea to take his dad's BMW for a bit of a spin. It wasn't."
fathom	**fa** [rhymes with have] thumb Understand. "Stinky had established that a cat, lavishly coated in blackcurrant jam and dropped upside-down from a height, will still land on its paws. Toast, on the other hand, will unfailingly fall jam-side down. Given that the cream colored lounge room carpet was still pristine (even if the cat was not), Stinky couldn't fathom why his mother was in a gargantuan funk.
forsaken	for **sake** en Abandoned, given up, left behind.
fugue	**fewg** Imagine one of those songs you did at school where one lot of you start singing 'dah dee do dah' etc etc and before you get to the end another group start singing the same 'dah dee do dah' etc, and then some others join in. Like

you're all singing the same song, but you start at different times.

gargantuan — gar **gan** chew an
Enormous.

glossary — **gloss** sar ree
A brief dictionary, explaining those words used in the book which might not be understood by all readers.

grotesque — grow **tesk**
Really ugly. Not just plain ugly but spectacularly ugly. So ugly that you take pictures of it and put it on your Facebook site so all your friends can laugh until they wet themselves.

habitat — **hab** it tat
The environment or home, where an animal or plant lives.

hieroglyph — **hire** oh gliff
Normally refers to the picture-like symbols used in ancient Egyptian writing. The meaning can be stretched to include writing that is hard to read.

hitherto — hi [as in hit] thir [rhymes with sir] **too**
Up until now.

hue	**hew**
	Color. "After drinking four vodkas, Ollie took on a greenish hue, and repaired to the bathroom, where he spent some time gazing mournfully into the toilet bowl."
ignoble	ig **no** bill
	A pain in the arse. Not honourable. It can also mean down the bottom of the pecking order, low in rank, not the chap you say: "Yes sir!" to.
ignominy	ig **nom** min nee
	Shame, disgrace, un-coolness. Ignominious means deserving or causing disgrace. If you suffered an ignominious defeat, you should crawl away and hide under a rock.
imbued	im **bewd**
	Filled with / soaked up in, a feeling or quality. "The cake I made for Mum's birthday looked a little wonky, but it was imbued with love."
imminent	**im** in nent
	About to happen. If you cross the street with your eyes closed, there's an imminent danger of being hit by a truck. Not to be confused with eminent, which means famous, respected, a big cheese.
incoherent	in ko **hair** rent
	Something said or written which cannot be

understood. "After Stinky Jones bit into the chilli sandwich which we had planted in his lunchbox, his mouth and throat seemed to burst into flame. He stuffed a banana in his gob to try and douse the fire, but it merely served to turn his shouts of abuse into an incoherent gurgle."

inebriated	in **nee** bree ate ted Drunk, pissed.
lavishly	**lav** ish lee Richly, profusely, generously. "Stinky Jones spread blackcurrant jam lavishly over the cat's back, then holding it upside-down a metre above the carpet, he dropped it to see whether it would land jam-side down, or on its paws. In so doing he risked his mother's disapprobation"
manatee	**man** a tee A big bloated-looking sea animal like a fat seal with floppy lips like a bull mastiff dog. Or, like a walrus without tusks. They weigh up to 600 Kg. Their closest relative is the elephant.
marvel	**ma** vill Without going into all that verb and noun stuff, this is one of those words where you could do it, or be it. To marvel means to be amazed. Being a marvel, means that you're amazing.

merit
: **mare** it
Deserve.

mermaid
: **mer** maid
Mermaids are not real - if you think they're real you're on drugs, and need help. The top half is a beautiful woman, and the bottom half is a fish tail - which must be inconvenient for all concerned. There is also a merman (a fishy bloke) - not to be confused with Ethel Merman, a singer from the old days.

mute
: **mewt**
Silent, speechless. "When Eddie Noon set fire to his trousers, passers-by stared at him in mute disbelief. Eventually one of them found a voice and asked: 'What the hell do you think you are doing?' to which Eddie replied: 'I'm burning my trousers.' Eddie thought the fellow must be an idiot, that he couldn't work that one out for himself."

oblivious
: oh **bliv** ee us
Unaware or unconcerned.

opprobrium
: a **pro** bree um
Criticism, bad things said, disgrace, un-coolness.

pachyderm
: **pack** ee derm
Elephant, or other large animal with a thick skin.

pastiche	past **esh**
	You'd think this was some sort of sticky, sweet pastry sort of thingy. Possibly with nuts. But no. It's art. It's when someone copies the style of some other painter or songwriter or some such arty type. Often a bit of a mixture of this and that. Sometimes it just means a big jumble bumble. It has nothing to do with pistachios -they're nuts.
pestilential	pesty **len** shall
	Usually this means harmful to crops, or to people, like a plague, but it can also mean annoying. If your bedroom is pestilential, its probably full of mice and fleas. (The term often implies there's lots of the nasty things, not just one mouse). "A pestilential influx of relatives at Christmas" means that they turned up by the busload - aunties who smell of garlic and pinch your cheeks, cousins who break your stuff, uncles who get drunk and pee on the veranda.
pristine	**priss** teen
	In its original condition; not messed with.
proselytise	pro **sell** it eyes
	Explain - usually in the sense of trying to make someone change their beliefs.

putrid	**pew** trid
	Having a nasty smell, like something rotting. Repulsive, revolting.
relocate	ree low **kate**
	Move somewhere else
rent	**rent**
	A large tear. Torn. "When Ollie's dad backed the car over the tent by mistake, quite a ruckus broke out: 'There's a rent the length of your arm' wailed his mother. 'The tent is rent' accused Ollie. 'Where's your sister?' asked his dad, looking pale, and they all peered gloomily though the rent into the tent."
ruckus	**ruck** us
	A commotion, shouting match, argy-bargy, quarrel.
S.A.S	Special Air Service
	Seriously fit army blokes, highly trained and disciplined to carry out the most dangerous and tricky military operations.
staccato	stuck **ah** toe
	A musical term for short sharp notes that don't run together. It is the opposite of 'legato' (which means smooth and flowing). Imagine saying: "tik tik tik tik" - that's staccato, whereas "laaaadeeeedaaaa" is legato. Don't say either of those things though, or they'll cart you away, you looney.

subterfuge	**sub** ter fewj [rhymes with huge] Deceit. A sneaky tricky bit of carry on, like when you tell Mrs Wotherspoon that Stinky Jones stole her pen, having planted the thing in his bag while he wasn't looking.
summonsed	**sum** munzd Demand that someone appear before you, right now. "When Mrs Jones discovered her smart-phone floating in the bath, she summonsed Stinky: 'Jeremiah! (which was his real name, which she used whenever she was really ticked off about something) I want a word with you now, please!' and she stretched out that 'please' word so far that it damn near broke. Stinky, fearing that he was in danger of being broke too, ignored her summons, and clambered out through his bedroom window, and made his escape down the drive."
surveys	sir **vayz** Look at something or someone carefully.
torpid	**tor** pid Lethargic, slow (mentally or physically), sluggish. If you described Freddie Bumstead as 'torpid' , then chances are he is a big fat lazy slob whose most intelligent utterance to date has been: 'huh?'"

tot	**tot** A small amount of an alcoholic drink such as whiskey, brandy etc (ie it refers to spirits rather than beer or wine)
turquoise	**turk** woyz Greeny blue (or bluey green)
wit	**wit** Intelligence. "Eddie Noon had sufficient wit to realise that setting fire to his trousers was best done when he wasn't wearing them."

By the same author:

www.ingramcontent.com/pod-product-compliance
Lightning Source LLC
Chambersburg PA
CBHW071318040426
42444CB00009B/2046